My Family and Me

Briendel Publishing
New Jersey

My Family and Me

by

Beverly Mach Geller

Second Edition 2012
First Edition 2012
Published by
Briendel Publishing
briendel.publishing@gmail.com

ISBN-13: 978-0615592343
ISBN-10: 0615592341

Printed in the United States of America

My thanks to
Anna Evans
Members of Delaware Valley Poets, Inc.
Members of U.S.1 Poets' Cooperative
David L. Harrison
My husband, Sam

Very special thanks to
    Nancy Demme

For all my little ones

Contents

My name is Samantha.
Come visit us
and stay awhile.

My Twin Brother, Adam

Sure, most twins look the same
like a pair of white socks
or two blue wool mittens.

My twin is different
'cause he's a boy.
So what? He's my best friend.

We collect toads and frogs
find fat worms and fireflies
have big burp contests.

At the seashore
we dig clams, build castles
race ahead of tumbling waves.

We have secret words
and share secret thoughts.

My Older Sister, Emma

People smile at Emma and say,
"What big blue eyes!
"What long lashes!"

They glance at me.
"And how are you today?"
I look down at the ground.

But when Mom says,
"You draw such amazing pictures,
and the colors are great!"

I feel beautiful.

My Little Brother, Blake

He smells so good
after his bath—
warm as sunshine
soft, smooth as silk.

I kiss his cheeks
his double chin
and hug him
head to toe.

Our Kitchen Turns White

Something strange
must hide in our house
and run about
when Mom and I
begin to bake
chocolate cake.

It waits until
flour fills the bowl,
then it tickles my nose
with its fingers and toes.

ACHOO!

Dad and the Monster

Tapping.
Snapping.
Something furry.
I'm scared.
Bang! It's coming closer.

Just in time, Dad
comes to my room
and shines his flashlight
into the night.
"Let's see what's making all that noise.

"The wind and rain
are playing games
with branches
of our big oak tree.
Look! That shutter's dangling."

Old Abner, monster cat,
runs into the corner.
When Dad begins to tuck me in
old Abner jumps in too.
We snuggle into sleep.

Aunt Sara's Bracelet Music

When I bake with my Aunt Sara
her bangle bracelets make me sing.

She sifts the flour—
flutes fill the air.
She stirs in eggs
our porch chimes peal

and her bracelets make me sing.

In goes sugar
brass bells tinkle.
When she pours milk
fiddles fiddle

and her bracelets make me sing.

She beats batter
drums beat, beat, beat.
Next come walnuts
banjo strings ping

and her bracelets make me sing.

Yellow batter
fills baking pans.
Oven doors close
as cymbals clang

and her bracelets make me sing.

I love to eat
the cake
but it's awesome
to hear Aunt Sara bake

while her bracelets make me sing.

Uncle Jake

Under our old oak tree
my Uncle Jake
bites a pear
with his big buck teeth—
a squirrel
nibbling on a nut.

Squirrels are furry,
Uncle Jake is bald,
but the way that he holds
the pear in his
—uh—paws
I see pointy ears and claws.

Grandma and Grandpa

In the rain we ride inside
the Holland Tunnel
when we visit
our Grandma and Grandpa.

Cars and trucks sing their songs
as we whiz-z-z along
under the river—there's no sky
under the river—we stay dry.

Our Dachshund

Sniff's our funny hot-dog dog
who stands on stubby sausage feet.

When he scoops up water
with his pink spoon tongue,
puddle to mouth
puddle to mouth
he never drips a drop.

I know how he can be so neat.

Because his legs are very short
his tongue is always near his feet.

Chocolate Ice Cream

When I lick my ice cream cone
and Adam makes me laugh,
soft chocolate ice cream
squishes out of my mouth
squooshes down to my chin.

But I don't care—
I wear an ice cream grin.

Surprise in Our Back Yard

A drake with a green neck
and a downy brown duck
swim side by side.

Later, he pokes his beak
into wet earth
looking for lunch.

They gobble up plump worms
then fold their legs
beneath wide wings.

Soon side by side
they swim again
in the muddy puddle
left from last night's storm.

Swans

Graceful sailboats
the swans glide through water
their feathers puffed with pride.

But on land they waddle
on clumpy legs
and their necks bob
up   up
   down   down.

So what
if I'm missing
my two front teeth?

Even the swans are not perfect!

Adam, Emma and I—Reflections

In our lake
tall trees grow downside up.
Green leaves hug the bottom
and brown trunks stand on top.

We feed the fish some bread—
they gulp without a sound.
Though our feet are on the ground
we see ourselves upside down.

Adam and I Watch the Party

Squirrels play tag
around the oaks
and hide and seek
among the leaves,
hang upside down
on swaying limbs,
or dig deep holes
with their big toes—
sticks, dirt, stones fly.
Six sit in a circle
munching mounds of acorns.

On crumbly brown leaves
we tiptoe closer—
grey heads pop up
bushy tails flick
whiskers wiggle
squirrels scatter.

Swallows

When Dad's truck horn blasts
clothespins on telephone wires
all fly away.

Hummingbird on Our Honeysuckle

An acrobat,
you fly up, down
poke your long beak
into honeysuckle
then fly backward, sideward
on fast fluttering wings
hum a song, pause,
sip more nectar
through your built-in straw.

Bird Talk

Bluebird whistles,
"I'll make a nest,"
while robins chirp,
"Fat worms are best."

Mockingbird sings,
"Today I'll teach
my little ones
to try their wings."

But then a jay
warns with his cry,
"A cat! Fly quick!
To the sky! To the sky!"

What I Hate Most—Collecting Eggs

A rooster guards
the hen house gate
and pecks my legs
'till I shoo him away.

When I grab eggs
from a hen's nest,
she tries to nip my hand.

My daily battle with chickens
would end
if only Mom
would buy eggs at the store.

My Delicious Dream

Last night I dreamt
that Adam, Emma and I
found a delicious field
filled with all our favorite foods:

chocolate trees
jelly beans on bushes
gum drops
caramels in high heaps
red lollipops
marshmallows crusty, hot
white and gooey inside
sixteen ice-cream sundaes.

I wish that Dad would plant
a candy field,
instead of the spinach
limas, squash and lettuce
tomatoes, potatoes
growing
row after row
after row
after
row.

Beach Days

I take my bath in a bathtub
and need a towel to get dry.
        but
we saw some gulls
stand on the sand
with wings spread wide
        to dry.

Since then, after a bath
my brother, Blake
        stands
and flaps his towel-wings
        till he's dry.

Rescue

Half-buried on the beach
white scallop shells hide.
Waves try to find them
and pound them to sand.

We take the shells home
in our pails—
white scallop shells
forever.

Bully

The bully
at school
is like a big bird
at the shore—
wherever it goes
little birds fly away.

Adventure Wishing with Adam

On the Sea of Wishes
we'll ride on a spouting
slippery whale.

We'll touch the tail
of a shy mermaid,
dodge a shark,
then dive down deep—
find sacks of gold.

We'll haul them home
and never, ever need
our allowance again.

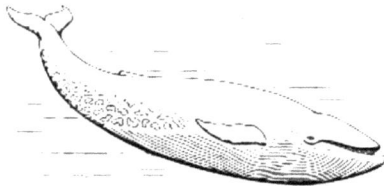

Scents of Rain

I love how the air smells
just before rain—
a plowed-field breeze
pine needles, piles of leaves.

I love how the air smells
just after rain—
honeysuckle so honey-sweet
cut grass, cut wheat.

Showers and Rainbows

On summer days
when clouds hang low
I wait
for them to overflow.

When wind's broom sweeps the clouds,
and sun's mop makes it dry,
rainbow ribbons
rest in the sky.

Our Oak in November

You look so bare and cold
old oak.
Do you need a coat
to keep you warm
            or
does the bark
that hugs you close
keep you warm
in wind and storm?

Winter Walk with Adam

Snow covers the back yard.
Our footsteps make a path.

We walk beneath an arbor
where roses used to climb—
the arch, a yawning mouth
our grill, a polar bear
our evergreens, sheep curled in sleep
forsythia twigs, like ears of wolves,
turn to the wind, listening.

Snowgirl

Feathery flakes
fall
on my nose
cheeks
coat
and boots.

I have
snow eyebrows
snow lashes
snow hair—
snow is stuck
on me everywhere.

No carrot nose
or pebble eyes for me!

I'm a snowgirl.

Almost Spring

At winter's end
the sad melting snow cries
a river of tears.

Spring Day with My Sister

We search
for a four-leaf clover

a robin
scratches earth
finds a rubber-band-worm

a brown sparrow
flies to her nest
straw in her beak

a fat bumblebee
in a black hat
buzz-zz-es by.

Spring celebrates
her birthday.

Sunset from Our Porch

Who pulls the string
on the red balloon sun
when it drops out of sight?

And where does that red balloon go
when it's tugged
from the sky?

And who sends the colors
that paint
goodbye?

What Holds Stars in the Sky?

When I was little
I wondered
what held the stars—
String?
Nails?
Glue?

Now that I'm big
I still don't know.
Do you?

My Star

When we're riding in our car
and night has put the sun to sleep,
I find the very first star.
It winks and follows me
as we ride home in our car.

About the Author

Beverly Mach Geller is a graduate of Syracuse University School of Nursing. After careers in nursing and interior design, majoring in English she earned a BA from Rutgers University and an MA from the College of New Jersey. Her poems for adults and children have been published in many literary journals and anthologies. She has received the Jane McHugh Memorial Senior Award for one of her poems. Her books for children include *The Shalom Zachar at Nachum's House, The Upsherin: Ephraim's First Haircut, The Mitzvah Girl, Ellie's Shabbat Surprise, The Mystery of the Missing Pitom*, and *Janice and Juanita*. She lives in East Windsor, New Jersey with her husband, Sam.

www.ingramcontent.com/pod-product-compliance
Lightning Source LLC
Chambersburg PA
CBHW071745020426
42331CB00008B/2185